THE
Archive Photographs
SERIES

CONSETT
THE SECOND SELECTION

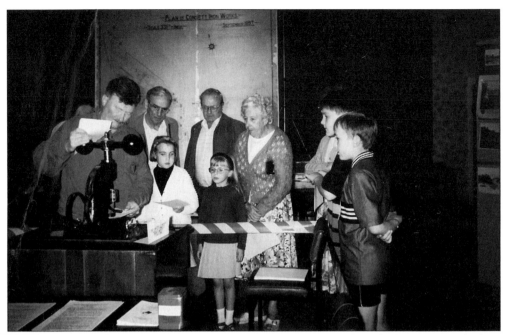

The Company Seal of the Consett Iron Company, being operated for the benefit of onlookers Orry and Kirsty Leslie and Andrew McGee and Ken McVickers during Derwentdale Local History Society's 1996 Year of the Visual Arts celebrations. Created in April 1864, the Seal was in use until the demise of the Company when it was nationalised in 1968.

The impression of the Seal, showing the Blast Furnaces, Mills and railway network of the early ironmaking industry at Consett, with the scroll of 'Consett Iron Company' surrounding.

THE
Archive Photographs
SERIES

CONSETT
THE SECOND SELECTION

Compiled by
Derwentdale History Society

CHALFORD

First published 1997
Copyright © Derwentdale History Society, 1997

The Chalford Publishing Company
St Mary's Mill, Chalford,
Stroud, Gloucestershire, GL6 8NX

ISBN 0 7524 1079 2

Typesetting and origination by
The Chalford Publishing Company
Printed in Great Britain by
Bailey Print, Dursley, Gloucestershire

Record breaking blast furnacemen at Consett in 1965. They achieved a record week's production of 7,000 tons of iron. The furnace in the background was designed in 1943 to produce 3,400 tons per week.

Contents

The Gamekeeper, thought to have been taken near to the River Derwent. The tools of the trade and apparel, which are rarely seen nowadays, offer a portrait and study in quiet professionalism and understanding of the countryside.

Introduction

Two years ago, when work began on the first in The *Archive Photographs* Series on Consett, no one could ever have imagined that the publication would go to a third reprint, and that requests for copies would come from every corner of the globe. In that edition emphasis was quite rightly given to the fact that the history and creation of much of what was the 'fabric' of Consett had something or other to do with the incumbent influences of the iron and steel and associated industries up until the beginning of the 1980s. This influence has continued for some well into the 1990s, while others, such as the younger generation born perhaps during and since the mid 1970s, may still feel the aftermath of the closure of the main employer in the area at the time. This may be recognised as a lack of certainty of their future prospects, as work, along with the deterioration of the economic base of the area, has continued to decline since the closure. For others the changes have been somewhat less bewildering with changing social patterns, causing many cinemas to close in favour of Bingo parlours and the like, and more pubs than one likes to remember having to close due to lack of custom. Or has this got something to do with not having to do shift work?

The beauty seen by many in the countryside of the Derwent Valley while the seasons change is no less dramatic than the changing patterns of commerce, from steel and dirt to light industry and tourism which attract many, but can hardly ever attract sufficient numbers of visitors from all over the world to make up for that loss of industry. The skyline as seen today is in its own way a similar one of say the early 1800s, before any industry appeared, and is today a far cry from that red and dusty skyline that many will remember. The lives and work surroundings of yesteryear have at times to be wondered at, as is the resilience and determination and indeed community spirit which comes through in many of the reflections in the book. The people of Consett township and area have long been noted for those attributes mentioned above, in particular that of being so remote from other parts of the district that others still seem to think, even today, that it always snows in Consett! But that very remoteness has borne in the people of Consett a spirit of independence and of common identity and knowledge of their neighbours and friends.

At the time when those very socio-economic forces which operated to cause the foundations of the town to be laid, and which caused thousands to come from every part of the United Kingdom, people and their progeny brought with them the very basis of each of their own, perhaps very differing cultures. These were unknown and unrecognised at the time as what they are today, the real social fabric of our area. These are Consett's strengths. The years have allowed not only the differing cultures to mellow but have allowed a careful blend of those attributes to emerge.

In this, the second selection of photographs, it was thought efficacious to dwell not only on the various industries of the area, but more on the people, the syndrome which many people only recognise as the ordinary 'plod on, lets get on with it, leave us alone, if just so that we can enjoy what is our life and work'. A feeling that all of us have at sometime or other. The Derwentdale Local History Society hope to have captured the odd moment of bygone days which will remind the reader, and anyone living in the Consett area, that theirs is an area that they can boast about and be very proud of, and will continue to do so for many years to come.

Editorial Committee
Tommy Moore, Norma Moore, Greta Armstrong and Gerry Armstrong

An aerial view of the intended Genesis Programme, formerly the steelmaking complex at Consett. Intended to regenerate the economic base of north west Durham, the site extends to over 700 acres which will eventually contain business parks, retail units, executive housing and a Synergy Centre. (Jefferson Air Photography Ltd)

One

A Glimpse at our Surroundings

Shakespeare Street, Consett in the early 1950s. Thought to be named, not after the Bard, but the Shakespeare Inn which was situated on the corner of Shakespeare Street and Raglan Street around 1920.

Two comparable studies of Newmarket Street, Consett, the main thoroughfare for traffic entering the town from Blackhill and Shotley Bridge. Above: Pre First World War. Below: Post Second World War.

Newmarket Street, Consett

An unusual view of Blackhill, showing Durham Road and the Presbyterian church prior to the housing constructions of St Andrew's Road and St Andrew's Crescent. Part of Durham Road and the Baptist church would eventually be built in the bottom left of the picture. Note the metalled road surfacing of Pemberton Road along the bottom of the picture.

Another view of the upper half of Durham Road in Blackhill. The metalled road surface of this arterial route between the historic cities of Durham and Hexham was once a toll road. Taken in Edwardian times, with the Victoria Inn on the left and horses being the main mode of transport, it gives the aspect of an unreal leisurely feel to life in those days.

11

Aynsley Terrace, Consett in the 1920s. A rare photograph as it shows the situation of both the water fountain on the left, and the Consett War Memorial in the middle background. The water fountain is now in the North of England Open Air Museum at Beamish.

Front Street, Castleside at the turn of the century.

Medomsley village taking in the then 'Stags Head' public house, presently a quite desirable cottage dwelling.

Snows Green hamlet near to Shotley Bridge. It is of quite ancient origins and is said to have been named after Thomas Snawe who once owned the land in the sixteenth century. The culverted waterway in the foreground was to carry the flow of the Tinkley Hill Gill which still runs (although now culverted) from the Consett Golf Course, through the hamlet and into the River Derwent some distance away.

Old Allensford Bridge before its demolition and more modern reconstruction in the 1920s. Although updated and modernised a number of times since then, the building on the Northumbrian side of the River Derwent, recently altered into quite desirable holiday homes, was formerly a farmstead and before that, a staging house known as the Castle Belsay Inn.

THE RIVER DERWENT DAM, SHOTLEY BRIDGE.

Water gauging and pumping station, River Derwent. Consett Iron Company was only allowed to pump a certain amount of water in any one day. The gauging station indicated how much water went over the dam and the flow of water. The water was pumped from the pump house at Howden into the works, and returned to the River Derwent down the Howden Burn after going through the companies' cooling towers.

The headstone reads; 'Here lyeth the body of Thomas Rawe of Wharnley Burn who departed this life January the 30th anno 1714 removed from Wharnley Burn 1866.' So reads the epitaph to Thomas Rawe, mosstrooper, desperado, freebooter, border reiver and thief. Rawe, who resided at Wharnley Burn Farm, lived in contempt and open defiance of the law of those troublesome days of the seventeenth and eighteenth centuries in the border counties. He escaped civil prosecution but was publicly excommunicated by the Church. The prohibition was read out in all local churches and in the market places of Hexham, Stanhope and Wolsingham. Being refused burial in consecrated ground, Rawe chose a spot under a tree on a beautiful premonitory which commands a view of all approaches and from which he is said to have used to spot his pursuers. The freestone slab was erected over his grave. When the farm changed hands the stone was placed in a wall of the farmhouse near Steeley, Satley. It is still there today, a memory of a local badman.

Van HaansBergen, a local magistrate at the end of the last century, and his mother outside their home at Five Lane Ends. Van HaansBergen, a Dutchman by birth, was a well known figure in the Consett area at the time.

Now long demolished, Mown Meadows farm croft stood opposite the Moorcock Inn at Waskerley. Little is known of the farm, although the family of farmer Joshua Gaskell (pictured) were shortly afterwards to move to the Tow Law area.

28 Snows Green Shotley Bridge Co Durham England

Aug 15/04

Would like a coloured view in exchange

G. D. Ridley

One of the forerunners of the Shotley Bridge General Hospital and North Durham Acute Hospitals Trust was Shotley Bridge Cottage Homes, seen here with the Derwent Valley to the west in the background.

An aerial view of the recently demised Shotley Bridge General Hospital, presently the North Durhams Acute Hospitals Trust. The former fully integrated hospital, which served the area for nearly fifty years, had its origins in the pre First World War need for care for the poor and eventually for the Second World War casualties, for which the prefabricated 'huts' were built in 1940. From 1948, Shotley Bridge Hospital was the third largest hospital in County Durham, offering health facilities to about 145,000 people.

The countryside to the south of Consett showing Hounsgill viaduct from this quite unusual angle and unlikely to be seen nowadays. The photograph was taken in July 1960 from the top of colliery waste heaps which were removed after the closure of the plate mill in 1979, along with the giant water cooling tower which serviced the plate mill at the time, to make way for Hounsgill Business Park. The Hounsgill viaduct, built in 1857 for rail transport, is presently a part of the Waskerley Way Country Park and is said to be ten feet higher than the High Level Bridge in Newcastle.

Consett Park was presented by Sir David Dale on behalf of the Consett Iron Company to the people of Consett in July 1890 and is presently administered by Derwentside District Council. In the background is St Aidan's church, an Ecclesiastical Parish from March 1884. The church was made redundant in early 1996. It was also built on land provided by Consett Iron Company and erected in 1885 by designs of Oliver and Leeson of Newcastle.

St Mary's R.C. Junior Mixed School, now demolished, was originally built for 120 children. The school was administered for many years by the Sisters of Charity. A reference is made on 16 August 1914 that 31 children were being transferred to the senior department. By 1966 this school was classified as a Junior Mixed School. St Mary's R.C. School was demolished due to vandalism and has presently been replaced by a modern open plan school on nearby Pemberton Road.

Blackhill cemetery, for the Ecclesiastical Parish of Benfieldside, comprises 11 acres and was formed in 1862. Originally under the control of nine members of a Burial Board, the two Mortuary chapels (or Chapels of Rest) allowed for the distinction of religions. The two chapels are presently Grade 2 listed buildings, with one being hallowed ground, and are presently under the administration of Derwentside District Council.

The parish church of St Cuthbert's of Shotley Bridge, erected in 1851 on land given by Thomas Wilson of Shotley Hall. The foundation stone had been laid on 7 March 1849. The church was built in the early English style consisting of a chancel and nave of five bays, aisles, transept and north porch and a tower with spire containing a clock and six bells. The adjoining Sunday Schools were opened in 1881.

Medomsley Hall, home and residence of the Hunter family for many years and later the residence of the County Court Circuit Judges when they sat in Durham Crown Court. The hall is presently a residential nursing home.

Two
The Social Side of Life

The Turf Hotel in Consett ran a splendid Chrysanthemum Show during the 1965 season. Here, Stan Capstick (middle) is posed with three others.

Almost every department in the Consett Steel Works held social evenings, this one was for Hownsgill Plate Mill Social Club, held in the Carlton in February 1971. The committee who organised the occasion was Gerry Armstrong, Bill Millhouse, Steve Richardson, John Murray, Eric Walls and Jacky Barratt. Among the members and guests were Messrs and Mesdames Derek Martin, J. Parkinson, Dicky Donaghy, Bill Postle, Kenny Halliday, and many more.

The Derwent Players gave this repertory production of *The Heiress* at St Aidan's church hall. Left to right: Betty Griffiths, Dorothy Byers, Edwin Hodgson, Alice Trewhitt, Edith Wake, -?-, Marjorie Hope, Tommy Burn and Muriel Howe. Unfortunately, the mists of time have clouded the identity of the young man fourth from the right. Other repertory groups which ran various productions during the 1930s, '40s and '50s included the Avenue Players and the Community Players.

Knitsley Cricket Club Dinner, 1950-51, held in premises at Middle Street, Consett. (Photograph by H. Freek).

The Avenue Girls' Brigade have always had a good following, here they are seen as a brigade marching along Medomsley Road, in the early 1950s, with their leader, thought to be Mrs Tate.

No one needs a further introduction to the Consett Steelmen Brass Band, conducted most successfully for many years by Mr Eric Cunningham.

A trip leaving the North Eastern Hotel, believed to be in the early 1950s. The landlord was Mr Pigg and the party included: Messrs Nicholson, J. Johns, P. Elliot, T. Rushgrove (both junior and senior), J. Scott, L. Young and others.

In 1966 St Mary's R.C. School Wind and Percussion Band took part in the music festival which was held every year at Consett Grammar School, now the Tertiary College.

This children's fancy dress competition at Castleside Show in 1961 show that a well organised annual show combined with bonny bairns and lively imaginations go down a treat!

A rare photograph of lads, led by Tom Brewis, ice skating on the reservoir dam on the River Derwent around 1925. The reservoir had formerly been used by the Annandale Paper Mills to which it was adjacent. When the Paper Mills closed it wasn't long before the locals used it for swimming in the summer and ice skating, as seen, in the winter. The reservoir was filled in for safety reasons in the early 1960s.

Air Training Corps Squadrons from the north sector competed at RAF Rufforth in late 1955 and the 1409 Consett Squadron team won a silver rose bowl outright for aircraft recognition. A few of the faces to be recognised are: Norman Harkness, Tony Curran, Denis White, Brian Murphy, Tommy Armstrong, Tommy Moore, Fred Stirling, Cyril Wilson, and Billy Arnott. A very dear friend and colleague who was always on hand to help and is well remembered was Tommy Taylor (extreme right, second from back).

It is 492 miles from Lands End to the area where these men and women called home! In 1958 Mr and Mrs E.W. Reed and Mr and Mrs G.H. Clinton were on holiday when this photograph was taken. Mr Reed, on the left, was a fitter and Mr Clinton was a scale car driver, both in the blast furnaces.

As popular as the present day pop groups were Ken Gray and his Orchestra, seen here 'swinging' in fine style. The orchestra had a large following in its heyday, which lasted many a day. The players were all very well known. They are, left to right: C. Ramsey, T. Winter, G. Winter, C. Ramsey, Ken himself, and Mr Bickle.

The darts and domino final for the Plate Mill sportsmen in 1967 when there were some very interesting games played. When the crane drivers won the darts title this photograph shows their enjoyment. Included are: L. Ridley, J. Walker, B. Rogan, R. Nixon, K. Thompson and Eric Jameson, amongst others.

Consett and Blackhill Park and Bandstand, c. 1890. The Consett and Blackhill Park was bequeathed to the people of Consett by the Consett Iron Company in July 1890. The bandstand is still well remembered even to this day but was dismantled shortly after the Second World War. Note the line of residential dwellings of Aynsley Terrace along the top of the photograph. These are no longer visible today because of tree growth.

Gus Robinson, Bob Saxty and Mr Browell enjoying their holiday camping at Allensford during the 1920s. The fourth person, on the left, is unknown.

These young ladies had every reason to smile, they had just taken part in 'The Battle of Britain' Beauty Queen competition in 1955 held in the Co-operative Hall in Consett. The winner was Miss Olive Maughan with Miss Audrey Stokoe of Moorside and Miss Ann Todd of Burnopfield second and third respectively.

Another occasion on which to celebrate was the annual gathering for the gifted thirty year service presentation in which workers and staff were rewarded for their long service in the iron and steel industry. Members of the fabrication department gathered in the Civic Centre for this presentation.

Builder George Carr Johnson takes his family for a drive in their 'Argyle', *c.* 1911. George was born at Iveston and his wife Sarah (nee Lennox) was born at Consett in 1869. Sarah was the sister of Ned Lennox, first bandmaster and one of four founders of the first organised Salvation Army Corps band in the world at Consett in 1869.

A queue of J.S. Robson's buses each bound for different destinations.

A party made up from members of the Royal Antediluvian Order for Buffaloes outside their premises at Station Road, Consett.

Three

Industry

The Railway Station at Blackhill was originally named the 'Benfieldside Railway Sidings', then Benfieldside Station in 1867. It was renamed Consett Station in 1882, and eventually fell to the name of Blackhill Station in 1886. It was closed to passenger traffic during the Beeching cuts in the 1960s and finally closed to all traffic by the mid 1970s. It is presently part of the Derwent Walk Country Park.

Poss Stick Mill, Ebchester

The Poss Stick Mill at Ebchester was owned by the Wardle family. Horses pulled the logs over the river by chains. The timber was brought from the Heugh Wood, Broadoak Farm to the mill to be fashioned into poss sticks which were used by the local women for possing cloths in the poss tubs. The mill was demolished in 1930.

SHOTLEY BRIDGE

The Railway Station at Shotley Bridge, opened at the same time as Blackhill Railway Station.

The Woollen Mill at Ebchester, also known as the Fulling Mill. In 1759 the mill was owned by Josiah Jewitt and Ralph Bainbridge and was a fulling and bleaching business, noted throughout the North. In 1874 it was owned by one George Moody. An advertisement of 1759 read as follows: 'Ebchester Blachfield, upon Derwent Water, 1759 Josiah Jewitt and Ralph Bainbridge in partnership, propose to carry on the bleaching of linen cloth at Ebchester as was carried on last year by Josiah Jewett'. Josiah Jewitt was buried in Ebchester cemetery in 1786.

In the bright early spring sunshine and against a background of leafless trees, these four statues of 'Founder members of the Durham Miners Association' make an imposing picture in Durham City. The statues are of Foreman, Patterson, MacDonald and Crawford. Although photographs may be limited in number and indeed in scope, the value and memories of the underground workers of the North West Durham area cannot be forgotten. Over thirty-seven collieries produced the finest coking coal in Britain. Perhaps this photograph can be seen as a fitting epitaph to those who worked in the industry.

In 1872 the flour mills owned by Mr Andrew Annandale were sold to the Co-operative Societies in the district and renamed 'The Derwent Flour Mill Society Ltd'. It continued to flourish until about 1930 when it was transferred to Dunston on Tyne. Note the steam-powered haulage wagon used to carry and distribute the corn and flour.

C.W.S.

FLOUR

DIRECT FROM YOUR OWN FLOUR MILLS.

WHEN ORDERING

C.W.S.

SELF-RAISING FLOUR.

The simplicity and direct approach of a good sales product needed no further advertisement than this.

A view of the steam engine road vehicle used so effectively before the internal combustion road vehicle became fashionable. Although slow by modern standards, early motor vehicles lacked that essential 'pulling power' which was provided by the robust sturdiness of the steam-powered engine.

THE STATION, HIGH WESTWOOD. 2338.

The new station at High Westwood was opened on 1 July 1909 and in its heyday over 132,000 passengers used the station. However, lack of demand caused its closure on 4 May 1942.

Probably the first lorry purchased by the Clydesdale family of Chopwell (Carriers) shortly after the First World War. Thought to be a five ton Leyland known as the RAF type. In the early 1920s Clydesdales ran one of the first bus services from Chopwell to Newcastle via High Spen. Parkers (also from Chopwell) ran another service to Newcastle via Hamsterley and Lintz Ford. Annie Bessford and Bob Brown ran from the Spen about the same time. For a while they were not allowed to cross Scotswood Bridge, although carriers and wagons could cross if empty but had to return via the Redheugh Bridge when laden.

The Railway Station at Rowley was built in response to the Stanhope and Tyne Railway of 1834 which passed 'Cold Rowley' as it was known in those days. Later the railway was to become the Stockton and Darlington Railway. Upon the closure of the station in the 1960s, the station was left derelict for some short time before being dismantled and transported to Beamish Museum where it is presently in use.

Man of Steel

A poem composed by Bill Johnson, based on the Consett Iron and Steel Co. prior to its closure.

Do you see that blood red glow my lad, lighting up the sky
Do you here that piercing whistle,
And that ghostly sounding cry?
Do you see that huge black mountain, hot lava streaming down,
And the billowing cloud of smoke and steam,
That ever hangs around?
Can you taste the rust-red dust my lad,
That settles on the ground,
Have you heard the clank of metal, and wondered at the sound?
Can you smell the acrid fumes my lad, and feel the searing heat,
Do you hear that hooter blowing and the tramp of heavy feet?
Are you sound in wind and limb my lad, and wish to earn your pay,
Have you left your schooldays far behind,
And no longer want to play?
Then this is the place for you my lad, you really have no choice,
Your father has toiled here all his life,
He speaks with the company's voice.
For this is a town of steel my lad, built on a moor-land hill,
Where iron ore was found galore, and its smelting goes on still.
This is where you'll work my lad, eight hours or more for days,
You'll sweat and toil with the rest of us,
And do what the gaffer says.
Don't you fret or worry my lad, you'll not be on your own,
For guiding you along the way, are men who do not moan.
They are men who started here, just like you do now,
With anxious thoughts and childhood fears,
That showed on furrowed brow.
Take note my lad, of what they say, they've done it all before,
Amidst the heat and screaming din, of steel born from the raw.
There's danger here, take care my lad, it's hot, its a noisy hell,
With belching smoke and fiery sparks, take heed and do not dwell.
Then one day you'll see my lad, a man you'll grow to feel,
An upright man, a working man, A Consett Man of Steel.

Looking south across the works blast furnace area, *c.* 1924. Although built many years before, the furnaces, stoves, chimneys, crane gantry, pig beds, ore and coke gears were all replaced about this time.

In an effort to keep Consett Steel complex a viable proposition, the transport of molten iron from Middlesbrough to Consett became a desirable feature. Although only achieving a moderate degree of success, the 'torpedo' trains began in August 1969 and travelled some 112 miles on a round journey. They were discontinued around 1971.

A view which many who worked or visited Consett Iron Company will remember. Looking from the west, with the Power Station on the left, the general offices (mid picture) and the three Blast Furnaces rising behind. The general offices were built from 1888 until 1891 and were the managerial and operational nerve centre of the works until closure.

The 'Valley' railway sidings at the top of the Grove and Moorside. The Grove Bridge is in the middle of the picture and the British Oxygen Plant, middle left. The importance of these sidings was to allow the smooth operation and flow of rail traffic throughout the Consett area.

Here, a 160 ton Roll Housing for the four High Mill is in transit through Consett on 28 April 1960. Excavated and the foundation laid in 1958, Hounsgill Plate Mill was the most modern in Europe when it was officially opened in April 1961.

One of the many shunting engines of the Consett Iron Company, used for many years to transport coal and steel throughout the area. Coal-fired engines were eventually phased out by about 1962 and replace by diesel locomotives.

The Consett Iron Company was world renowned for their research and development programmes, although sometimes they had no objection to following a new product line. This advertisement of the time shows this very fact.

From 1834 until 1984 there had been a rail service to and from Consett. Firstly by the Stanhope and Tyne Railway (1834), then the N.E.R. and finally by British Rail. In December 1984 the last train (pictured) was to run from Consett Railway Station. The train was laid on to commemorate event which was organised by Derwentside Rail Action Group.

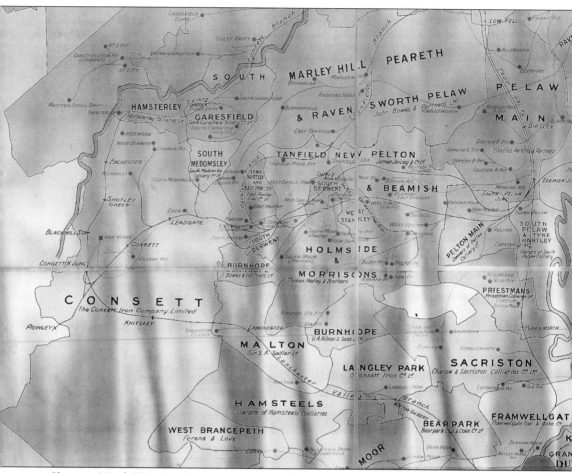

Showing North West Durham as a part of the Durham coalfield, depicting the historic position of the coal pits and railways serving the district.

The Durham Big Meeting in the early 1950s. The banner of the Beamish Mary Colliery is in the background. In the foreground is the colliery manager, Joe Mains.

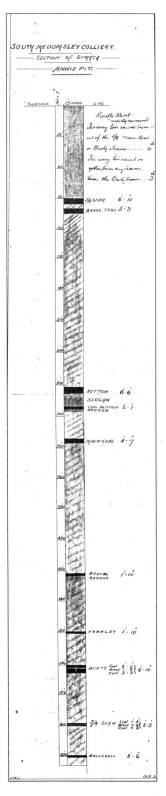

The section of strata of the Dipton/Leadgate area of North West Durham. It gives some indication of the claustrophobic conditions and depths within the earth that coal miners often worked. As a brief example, a pit near to South Medomsley, the Eden Pit, produced 4,362 tons from the 5/4 seam and 4,610 tons from the Hutton seam in the November/December period of 1910.

The Slab Bloom and Billet Mill was opened around 1953, and as the name suggests, produced many products for industry. After the steel ingots had been 'stripped' from their moulds, the still red hot and malleable steel ingot was weighed before being processed into a saleable commodity. Here a twenty ton ingot is being weighed off prior to being rolled to slab size.

The Oxygen Steelplant charged up to 120 tons of molten 'hot metal' or molten iron into a L.D. vessel with each charge. Besides the hot metal, the vessel was also charged with cold scrap steel to add to the hot metal, making it possible to make up to 160 tons of high grade steel in as little as 50 minutes. The last L.D. to be erected in the works was the L.D. 4 and was first blown on 18 July 1973. L.D. or Linz-Donowitz, the Austrian town from where the process was derived, was further researched and developed by Consett Iron Company for many years.

The Fell Coke Works was opened in 1928 and produced many by-products besides coke; such as benzine, naptha and tar. The plant was upgraded on a number of occasions. The photograph shows a 'charge' of about 150 tons of red hot coke being pushed from the coke ovens. This would then be quenched and screened prior to sale or use.

The entrance to the Consett Steel Works after the closure in 1980. A view taken not far removed from the present site of Safeways Superstore, looking west. Note the Power Station (opened in 1949) mid-picture to the left, water cooling towers (opened 1948-49) mid-right and the Oxygen Steelplant in the background. This area has presently been renamed, as part of the Genesis programme, the Ponds Court Business Park.

A view towards Consett from the top of the Grove and Moorside Bank with the coke works' fuel bunkers on the right and the blast furnaces just visible on the left. This road, which once meandered its way through the complex virtually cutting it in half, was once known as the 'Healyfield to Dipton Road' during the early nineteenth century, as the town of Consett had at the time hardly come into existence. The railway, which ran under the bridge, has since disappeared to make way for more open grassland and space.

The steelmaking ladle being charged with the finished steel product. Note the additions chutes just above the ladle. These allowed finishing ferrous and non-ferrous additions to be made to the finished steel to the requirement of the customer specification.

Following the closure of the Consett steelmaking complex in September 1980 the eventual demolition work began. Local comedian Hughie Malone said at the time: 'It's all over Lads, you've had the best, now they say you can have the rest, I was asked to switch the lights off, but I cannot find the switch!'

Four
People at Work

The woman at work is Mrs Rachael
Foreman who lived in Consett. Doing the
washing for sixteen people was no easy task
as washing with a poss tub was dreadfully
heavy work. The photograph is a reminder
of the sheer hard graft and grind of being a
housewife until quite recent years.

The Derwent Livery Stables, conveyances for hire. The proprietor was G.E. Glendinning. Little is known of the premises from which this local business operated, however, the fashion of transport and dress are quite unique, as they each have changed with the progress and advances made by the local haulage firm.

This car was a 1908 Armstrong Whitworth. The quiet distinction of the vehicle was that it was one of the first of its kind in the Consett area and was owned by Dr Bratton. The driver was Mr Billy Mullen who drove the post van for the Consett Iron Company for many years. Dr Bratton can be seen in the section 'Sports and Recreation'.

The British Red Cross Society and the St John Ambulance were grateful recipients when this new ambulance was presented by the British Steel Smelters Mill, Iron, Tinplate and Kindred Trades Association, *c*. 1905.

Mr George Richardson, chauffeur to Sir Edward George and the Consett Iron Company for many years. An informal moment on Medomsley Road, Consett for a sometimes greatly demanding job.

Character and cheerful purposefulness seem to give an aura of intent from these men in the pre First World War era.

C.I. Co. Ltd, Pattern Shops, 1937. Many faces will be well remembered from this portrait.

Thought to have been taken shortly after the end of the Second World War, the men and women of the company's scrap gantry beside the Fell Coke Works. Included, among others, are: Billy Moss, Stewart Sayers, Billy Mahoney, Kate Reilly and Florrie Wheatley.

Taken from the Blast Furnace top looking east and north. The platers, welders and acetylene burners look in good spirit perched about fifty feet above ground level. The cooling towers are in the background with Consett housing in the middle of the picture. Note the auxiliary diesel engine house to the left of middle. This was later bought and remodelled as a quite desirable residence in the late 1980s – near to Ponds Court Business Park.

The cycle of work, or when and how often a worker is seen to do an act of production or manufacture, is belied by the sheer scale and immensity of this the No. 1 Kaldo main frame assembly in the Oxygen Steelplant in March 1963. Weighing approximately 260 tons, great care and precision at every stage of operation was vital to the success of the completed construction.

A familiar figure for many years in the Consett area was Toux Hamon of Brittany who started coming to the district to sell his onions in 1908. More familiarly known as 'Peter' he made a host of friends and found the people of North West Durham very hospitable.

A training exercise of the gas rescue team at the Blast Furnaces, Consett. The ever-present hazard of toxic fumes and gases meant that safety teams were always kept in readiness were there to be a need for their skills.

A little known fact is that the Consett Iron Company had its own ambulance team long before any National Health Service was thought of. Here is the old Fell Coke Works ambulance team in the late 1920s. Back row, left to right: K. Almond, J. McElhone, and C. Chester. Front row: J. Phillipson, C. Brown and J. Westhope.

These four men, photographed in 1957, had 215 years service with the Consett Iron Company between them. The are, left to right: Thomas Stewart (51 years), Mr J.E. Bell (56 years), Mr G.H. Turnbull (58 years) and Mr R.J.N. Winter (50 years).

Taking a final analysis by sampling the as yet untapped charge of molten steel was a vital operation to ensure customer satisfaction in the Oxygen Steelplant at Consett. Here, Reginald Lowdon of Castleside spoon samples steel from an L.D. convertor prior to the steel being tapped out into a ladle.

Here is an old group at the Fell Coke Works. The men and boys are named as far as possible. Included are: J.D. Eath, R. Rudd, W. Ellis, S. Heaviside, R. Sherriff, W. Robson, J. Hannon, C. Browne, T. Harrison, A. Elliott, J. Callaghan, J. Gallagher, H. Clark, R. Mitchell, T. Francis, J. Hetherington, R. Wyatt, T. McAleer, T. Martin, J. Wyatt, J. Willis, G. Bell, W. Dent, W. Stafford.

This photograph is thought to have been taken during the mid 1960s, the men include: crane driver Alan Morgan, stripper crane driver 'Butch' Robson with electricians mates Ken Dickenson and Dennis Aubrey.

Bill Johnson (left) and Clive Pooley, two seventeen-year-old Consett Iron Company apprentice pattern makers in 1948.

Telephone operators in Consett Iron Co. exchange in 1957. Included are: Mrs H. Ruddick, H. Dixon, N. Roberts, Mr K. Charlton and standing is Miss. E. Charlton.

Bart Harwood was a well known trade union organiser in the Plate Mill for many years. He worked for over forty years on the overhead cranes. This presentation on his retirement was attended by many work colleagues, including: Gerry Armstrong, Joe Lawson, Willie Postle, Tom Bell, Bill Anderson, Geordie 'Bash' Wilkinson, Tommy Thompson and loading bay supervisor Ray Dinning. Mr Harwood was also a Methodist Lay Preacher for many years.

An induction of future operatives at the British Steel Corporation, Consett Works during the 1970s. Many young men became fully trained operatives in a number of disciplines while being employed at Consett.

Lowson Westgarth's employees working at Castleside, 1909.

Langley Park builder John Johnson altering a shop in 1909. John Johnson was a very successful businessman and prolific builder in North West Durham.

In 1953/54 the Shotley Bridge Junior School at Snows Green was being constructed by this team of workers. The photograph shows them gathered around the foundation stone of the school. Included are: Tommy Watson, Frank Bradley, Derek Oliver, Norman McKinnel, Keith Collingwood, 'Tess' Wilson, Tommy Kennedy and Fred and Billy Yarrow. In charge was Tommy Reece (centre front).

Five young local men became trainees at the N.C.B. training centre at Kibblesworth in 1958/59.

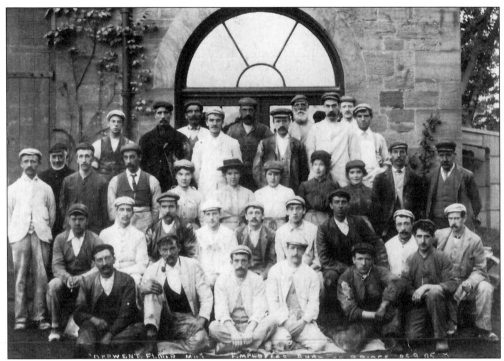

The men and women who worked at the Derwent Flour Mill, Wood Street, Shotley Bridge, 1905.

Haymaking at the turn of the century. Miss Hill lived in Forge Cottage at Shotley Bridge at the time. Included are: Jack Carruthers, Bob Hall, Bill Stokoe, Tommy Carruthers, Nellie Carruthers, Bill Turnbull and Mrs Lister.

Thought to be staff and workers from the J.S. Robson's garage and bus service in Blackhill.

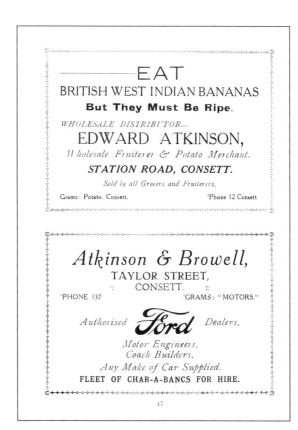

These two Consett businesses are still well remembered in the area to this day.

This photograph, and especially the faces therein, remind the reader of the privations and hardships sometimes endured to gain the rights of people at work. We respectfully offer thanks to everyone both living and dead for those efforts on behalf of us all.

Although rarely seen on the main streets of Consett, trade unionism and support for workers' causes still got the support from time to time as this march along Medomsley Road opposite the old Consett Market Place shows.

Local residents of Consett buying their greengroceries from Mal Edwards on Consett Market. Mal still has a stall on the market which is now held in Middle Street.

Taken opposite the Freemasons' Arms at Consett. The dress style suggests that this was the 1950s reminding us that 'work' is a term of which there are many interpretations. The thoughtful expressions of the bargain hunters looking for a 'good buy' show that market day has changed little.

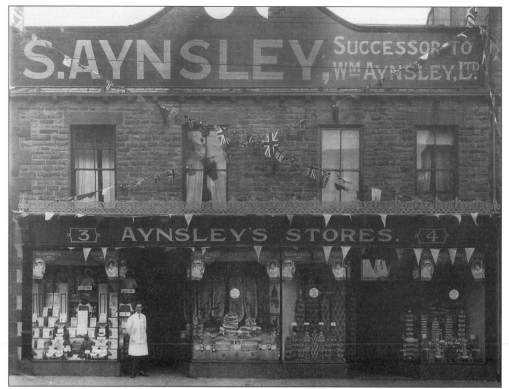

Sid Aynsley's of Middle Street, Consett, a well know business family for many years. The prices indicated in the shop windows would make a modern shopper quite envious.

George Courtney cycles and wireless dealers. During the period between the two world wars, and until the growth in popularity of car ownership, cycling was, and still is for many, a very popular outdoor pursuit.

A fore runner of the modern day 'super store', this photograph of the men and women who worked for Broughs General Dealers at the corner of Sherburn Terrace and Station Road, Consett during the 1930s certainly brings back many memories of yesteryear. Note the price of the hams in the window.

DRAPER **R. C. FOSTER** OUTFITTER

FOSTER'S

The Noted Shopping Centre for
Consett & District,

With a 43 Years' reputation.

**For Ladies' & Children's Outfitting of
every description.**

Men's, Youths' and Boy's Clothing,
Tailor Made Suits. Perfect Fit Guaranteed.

Specialists in Irish Linen Goods, Ladies' Cashmere and
Silk Hosiery, "Own Knit" Socks and Stockings
and our "own make" Shirts.

R. C. FOSTER, Progressive Store,
THE

CONSETT.

1

The advertisement tells it all, except that the premises were in Middle Street, Consett!

Dave Coxon of Shotley Bridge proudly exhibits his gun and dog in the 1920s.

Christmas Morning.

A postal delivery on Christmas day! The dress and uniform of those depicted on this old photograph offer a rare insight into life much earlier in this century.

Five

Serving Our Country

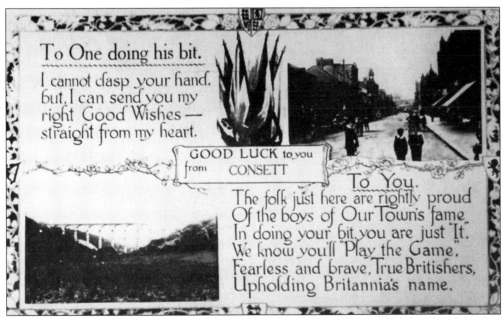

To One doing his bit.

I cannot clasp your hand,
but, I can send you my
right Good Wishes —
straight from my heart.

GOOD LUCK to you
from CONSETT

To You.
The folk just here are rightly proud
Of the boys of Our Town's fame,
In doing your bit, you are just "It",
We know you'll "Play the Game",
Fearless and brave, True Britishers,
Upholding Britannia's name.

Memories of good wishes in hard times for the lads of Consett in the First World War abound in the above.

Four soldiers of the 8th Battalion Durham Light Infantry, Royal Military Police outside their tent during the First World War.

Hughie Malone, one of eight brothers of the same family that served in the First World War. Hughie was killed in the Dardanelles but the other brothers returned safely home.

Wounded soldiers of the First World War convalescing at Whinney House were often invited with their nurses to the Annual Garden Party held at Shotley Hall, just outside the village.

Volunteers of Consett Drill Hall during the First World War.

For many years this First World War tank was sited just off Aynsley Terrace in the park, placed there in memory of those who fell during that conflict. Unfortunately, it was taken to aid the war effort during the Second World War. Natty Draffan is seen in front of the tank.

German prisoners of war clearing the land at Shotley Bridge in 1919. Shotley Bridge Hospital was used for war casualties during the First World War.

A Shotley Bridge welcome home. Captain Priestman presents the Military Medal to Corporal Telford.

The ladies of Shotley Bridge welcome home committee, 27 September 1919.

Some of the medal awards of the Second World War.

Men England Forgot

Now this is a story of men in their glory,
Who fought in the desert all bloody and gory,
They think of Old England, who thinks of them not,
And they go by the title 'Men England Forgot'.
They live in their sandholes just living their lives,
Dreaming of Old England, sweethearts and wives,
They are fed up with shellfire, shrapnel & shot,
For they know in their hearts they're 'Men England Forgot'.
They are out in the desert with sand storms all day,
Left all behind them good jobs and good pay,
But shall they worry who cares who gets shot,
What's the odds anyway, they're 'Men England Forgot'.
They have lived with their sorrows, heartaches and fears,
But those who fight with them could tell us a lot,
Hardships gone through by 'Men England Forgot'.
This is the end of my story, of men who died in glory,
The sons who have fought,
And the sons who were taught,
By the 'Men England Forgot'.

Sergeants and Warrant Officers of HQ Coy 2nd Battalion DLI in India, 1942. These included many soldiers from North West Durham: Sgts Hill, Robson, Philipson, Maddison, Harland, Brannigan, Proud, Campbell, McGlen, McBeth, Smith, Starkey, Walsh, Gunn, Ward, Thompson, Farrow, Cockburn, Morton and Wilds. Wilkinson, Noble, Crozier, RQMS Usher, RSM Hogg, CSM McCourt, CQMS Crawford, Sgt Hogbin and Robinson and Griffiths.

Many will remember Doug Wray, a popular local comedian and journalist. Doug is seen here during his war years in the South East Asia Theatre of Operations sketching Prime Minister Winston Churchill. Others may remember Doug doing the same sketch at the V.E. celebration concert at the Empire Theatre in Consett in May 1995.

The 2nd Battalion DLI Shotley Bridge Home Guard, 1940-41. Cyril Wilson is in the second row, far right.

The 3rd and 4th Battalion, the Consett and Lanchester Homeguard, on a training weekend at Brancepeth Castle, 1941.

These brave ladies of the ARP, in 1941, prepare for their duties in the 'Mams Army of the Day'.

Lads of the 10th Battalion DLI Army Cadet force (Consett) at muster after returning from Summer camp, c. 1956.

The ever popular Njimegan march, Holland, July 1989, a four day march covering over 100 miles. Among those present were L/Cpl, Hall and Renwick, Sgt Rearson, L/Cpl Eagle, Cpl Spencer (team medic), trooper Moore, Cpl Blades and L/Cpl Wilde. By the late 1960s the 17th Battallion the Parachute Regiment (TA) was amalgamated with other regiments to form the 4th (Volunteer) Battalion, the Parachute Regiment (TA).

'Grub Up' with 17 Battalion, the Parachute Regiment. Standing, left to right: Tony Grant, Jimmy 'Irish' Boyle, Brian 'Spud' Murphy. Sitting: Colin Laverick, Peter Grant, -?-, Bob English, Bob Brown and John Todd.

Members of 'C' Company, 17 Battalion, the Parachute Regiment (TA) at Consett Drill Hall when they were about to leave for their annual camp. In the year in question this was at Okehampton in Devon. Included are: J. Todd, H. Peacock, A. Hughes, L. Smith, N. Taylor, P. Grant, J. Boyle, G. Foreman, K. Miligan, A. Vickers, B. Devanney, A. Golightly, B. Brown, R. Sharp, A. Eddy, D. Mannion, I. Gill, A. Kirk, T. Grant, C. Nixon, G. Higham and C. Laverick.

Civil defence volunteers try out an improvised derrick. Following the Second World War, the importance of civil defence to the general population in the event of a nuclear conflict was quickly realised. To deal with this crisis, industry throughout the country formed themselves (with Government assistance) into civil defence units both to protect the population and wherever possible to keep manufacturing industry in production. Consett Iron Company played a major part in many of the various activities related to civil defence.

CONSETT WAR MEMORIAL.
Unveiled on Sunday, Sept. 30th 1923, by Major General
F. A. Dudgeon C.B., G. O. C. 50th (Northumbrian) Division

Wilson - Clarance

'In finality, not only 'Lest we forget' but more especially that they never be forgotten'. Consett's First World War Memorial was unveiled on Sunday 30 September 1923 by Major General F.A. Dudgeon C.B. G.O.C., 50th Northumbrian Division. Sadly the Second World War came along and added many more names to the ones already listed.

A scene on Consett Market Place around 1960. Robert W. Walker, a part-time student at Consett Technical College at the time, was being told all about the good life in the army by Sgt A. Leybourn of Crookhall who was on leave from the Royal Tank regiment.

Six

The Best Years of
Our Lives

All decked out in their summer clothes and dresses are children at Castleside vicarage 'Garden Party', 9 July 1912.

An extension of ribbon dancing can perhaps be seen in the much more ancient Maypole dance, seen here being performed at the turn of the century.

Young children always enjoy a game, they knit the fabric of socialisation which is important to everyone of us. Here we have ribbon dancing being performed by five to seven year olds.

FINGER OR THUMB?

These children look happy playing in the school yard. Although many children's schoolyard games are long gone, and sadly little remembered nowadays, the game of 'Mount a Kittie, Mount a Kittie, Finger or Thumb', the children's guessing game of the 1930s is still recalled.

It may have been advisable to keep well wrapped up against the cold when this photograph was taken. It's that unforgettable game of 'muggles' or marbles to the grown-ups.

St Mary's R.C. School football team after winning the cup in 1935. Back row: H. McArdle, Williamson, McGurk, Meegan, Hurrel, McCourt, Lisle and M. Slavin. Middle row: Father Treach, Boyle, Glasgow, Watchhorn, McCable, Brady and Father Holliday. Front row: P. Glancy and W. Luck.

Consett County Junior School football team. These lads were the league runners-up in 1951-52. They are: teachers Mr H. Moore and Mr R. Spanton. Back row: R. Fife, F. Roe, W. Stoddart, J. Dyson, J. Rutherford, J. Proctor, R. Barron. Centre row: D. Sanderson, R. Armstrong, L. Jeffery, J. Siddle, R. Tomkinson. Sitting: I. Chisholm and B. Richardson.

Consett Girls School hockey team was very well supported in 1916.

Consett swimming baths has had lots of good swimmers in their pools. The three youngsters shown here in the 1960s did remarkably well in competitions. They are, right to left: Joy Raisbeck, Paul Starforth and Brian Nixon.

Consett Grammar School prize winners, 1936. This photograph was taken in three parts and that is why some faces appear more than once. Included are: Daisy Hodgson, Miss Copplestone, Dr Spurdle, Aaron Dixon, Dorothy Mordral, Miss Wilson, Mr French, Mr Hughes, Gertie Nichols, Madame Hall, Miss Wilkinson, Miss Tweddle, Leila Walker, Vera Bird, Billy Fletcher, Delores Laurent, Norah Martin, Betty Smith, Mr Thornton, Alister McKenzie, Albert Jackson, Godfrey Briggs, Harold Bell, Ada Hutchinson, Norah Bell, Kathleen Horsfield, Marjorie Cotterill, George Smith, Gunnion, Ida Jennison, John Roberts, Iris Congleton, Ralph Boyle, Jean Parker, Alan Scott, Doris Askew, Bill Walker, Margaret Little, Miss Crowley, Mr Jones, Mr Briggs, Elizabeth Loughran, Dorothy Bainbridge, Jack Edgar, Norman Armin, Olga Johnson, Frank Routledge, Marion Pearson, Mr Canning, Mr Williams, Lorna Dyson, Fred Buckle, Dorothy Shaw, Betty Fletcher, Mr Bradley, Nellie Smith, Duncan Reekie, Muriel Richardson, Charles Percival, Miss Lawson, Miss Dixon, Miss Straw.

How many do you remember?

Little is known of this study, other than to say the children were photographed at the 'Wishing Stone' in Blackhill Park in the early 1950s.

St Aidan's scouts all prepared for summer camp. Included are: John Williams, Roland Wood, Michael Woods, Stephen Scott, David Stableforth, Wallace Greener, John Storey and John Collins.

Boys and Girls of Consett Junior School, 1961-62. Back row, left to right: headmaster Mr Howard, N. Green, W. Hutchinson, C. Gibb, E. Anderson, I. Stephenson, R. Reed, M. Peacock, B. Poole, J. Parker. Middle row: M. Mitchell, A. Colbourn, L. Moore, G. Dobbins, H. Bell, J. Maxwell, S. Nicholson, M. Hirdman, M. Byers, L. Kitchen, V. Lynn, M. Thomas. Front row: L. Lambton, J. Rowell, I. Dodds, L. Prosser, B. Elliott, B. Warrington, Miss Errington, A. Beatie, C. Cummings, P. Henderson, J. Thompson, J. Hill and H. Collins.

These little girls were pupils at St Patrick's School, c. 1917. To the right is Canon John O'Donoghue and on the left Miss Peggy Boyle.

Senior girls from Consett Grammar School who passed the scholarships in 1931. Back row, left to right: Jean McKay, Doris Askew, Helen Whitter. Front row: Jenny Williamson, Muriel Richardson, Ada Hutchinson, Elsie Milner, Freda Simpson.

Pupils of Consett Junior Mixed School in 1955. The teacher is Mr Legg.

Mr Kempton was the headmaster at Consett Council School when these food parcels were being prepared for distribution to the elderly in the 1970s. Included are: J. Graham, K. Thompson, P. McCulley, S. Niffton, L. Morecroft, L. Pulman, and B. Moss and Messrs R. Elliot, J. Bainbridge, D. Nixon, A. Douglas, B. Edgar, S. Bell, K. Dixon and Mrs M. Howe.

The obligatory 'school photograph' sometimes highlights and accentuates the quiet hope and acceptance as seen in the faces of these proud children, who pose in Consett Council Children's Choir.

This play school was held in St Aidan's church hall in 1977. The play leader was Mrs Margaret Gwillym (centre back), seen here at the Christmas party. Mrs Lynn Thompson (left) and Mrs Janet Chilton (right) were helpers of the play school. Among the children are: E. Moore, R. Thompson, P. McArdle, C. McCullough, A. Peacock, I. Parkinson, W. Brown, M. Porter, S. Chilton, D. Norman and J. Brown, J. Davison, G. McGuigan, S. Rudd, L. Jenkin, P. Dixon, J. Miller, P. Gash, A. Johnson, K. Parkinson, T. and M. Morris, S. Heslop and L. Brittan. Mr Billy McKean was Santa Claus.

A class from Blackfyne Comprehensive School, *c.* 1977.

Father J.F. Kennedy and Sister Colette of Our Lady of Immaculate Conception, St Mary's R.C. church in Blackhill with a class of first communicants. Among the communicants are: J. Bell, T. Lavery, Brown, A. Cant, C. Page, C. Murphy and C. Williams.

The Consett Salvation Army Junior Band members at the doors of the citadel in 1954. Included are: Gordon Curtis, Derek and Barry Raine, Brian Stoddard, and the surnames of Coulson and Parnaby.

Consett Iron Company held
many competitions throughout
the departments, one being a
snapshot competition. This
delightful shot won first prize for
T. Davies who worked in the
lubrication department in 1959.

Young and old alike, there's no distinction where a good game of 'Hoops and Girths' were
concerned.

Seven
Sport and Recreation

Castleside Albion AFC, Durham FA junior cup competition, 1908-09. Castleside did well to be runners-up in this hectic season.

Local stars of yesteryear are featured here with Consett AFC, 1895-96. Back row: J. Bowen (trainer), T. Robinson, F. Kempster, C. Pescod, C. Ternbent, A.E. Kempster (secretary). Middle row: J. Brown, J. Carruthers, R. Wake. Front row: J. Sisterson, A. Frosdick, R. Robinson, P. Smith, R. Harkness (captain).

Castleside Albion football team, 1912-13. Along the back row, not wearing football kit are: J. Pattison (secretary), D. Harkness, Clarke, K. Storey, A. Toward, B. Davison, A. Raine. The team were: Goalkeeper: W. Storey. Full Backs: J. Hull, E. Proud. Half Backs: C. Hopton, M. Buchan, E. Graham. Forwards: W. Bewick, P. Williamson, A. Johnson, J. Harkness, W. Raine.

In the 50th Jubilee year of Durham Football Association in 1933, Blackhill AFC was the winning football team. Back row: J. Finnigan, P. Freeman, J. Savage, R. Elliot, M. Slavin, G. Benson. Front row: J. Martin, J. McElrue, A. Blight, ? Chambers and O. McGinn. A Short History of Blackhill AFC includes:

1931-32 Harelaw Aged Miners' Cup, Gateshead Charity Cup
1932-33 League Challenge Cup
1932-33 Durham Amateur Cup
1932-33 N.W. Durham Amateur Cup

St Cuthbert's Parish church football team, 1925. There were many Consett Iron Company connections, and here are a few of them: Eddie Ward (fitting shops), Bob Lishman (pattern shops), Norman Siddle (traffic), W. Foggon (accounts), Cecil Wilson (pay dept), Maurice Wilson (timekeeper), Wilhelm Proud (secretaries) – Mr Proud was one time mine host at the Commercial Hotel in Consett – J. Roxby Surtees and Fenton Surtees (blast), Jack Surtees, Jack's father Jack Surtees (masons) and J.R. Surtees snr.

FOOTBALL MATCH.

CONSETT IRON COMPANY, LIMITED.

Pay Department Challenge Cup.

MARRIED v. SINGLE

(Holders)

To be played on

Vicarage Field, Consett,

On Wednesday, 28th Sept., 1927.

Kick-Off - 6 p.m.

Proceeds in aid of Consett & District Nursing Association and St. John's Ambulance.

TICKETS - 3d. EACH.

Consett & District Nursing Association and the St John Ambulance Brigade showed a novel form of fund-raising in this ticketed football match during the 1920s.

Consett Iron Company boasted a junior football team for many years. In 1957-58 season they had a very successful year, although they were beaten in the final of the cup competition. Back row: left to right: M. Hutton, A. Bellamy, K. Lowes, R. Cleghorn, R. Walton, F. Porteous, P. Richardson. Front row: A. Bollands, J. Dukes, W. Spedding, B. Smithson.

Young aspiring footballers of the Consett area. Included are: Norman Smith, Billy Wilkinson, Austin Lee, Doug Oxley, Keith Temperley, M. Young, L. Boyle, Brian Barsby, ? Thompson and John Stelling.

The 'also rans' were the Blowhard vs the Shortwinds rugby team in the 1920s. The names include: Ernie Wilson (the Barber), Fred Surtees, two Raisbeck brothers, Frank Barron and 'Pom' Urwin.

Consett Cricket Club's first eleven in 1912. It shows the senior eleven and club officials with a trophy won in that year. They played in the heyday of the club and established many records. Back row: A. Simpson, A. Brodie, H. Dyson, J. Siddle, J. Wilson. Middle row: J. Askew, G. Hamilton, H. Henderson, J. Eltringham snr (reserve), W. Buckett, W. Collinson, P. Freeman. Front row: Gus Robinson, A. Oliver, H.L. Dales, J.J. Eltringham jnr, J.H. Best, T. Houston, W. Miller.

Consett and District cricket team. Although the date of this photograph is uncertain, those who can be identified appear on several others in this book. These players were: 1. C. Turnbull (umpire), 2. Alf Hurst, 3. Joe Eltringham, 4. Johnny Best, 5. G. Hamilton, 6. Percy Freeman, 7. Hon. secretary – name unknown, 8. Alf Oliver, 9. Gus Robinson, 10. Jack Raine (captain and Consett post officer), 12. Bob ?, Shotley Bridge, 13. Wicket keeper – name unknown, 14. L.W. Coates.

Consett rugby team. Back row: Jackie Brown, Billie White, Wally Nixon, Fred Garven, John Peel, Jack Ross, Geo. Hetherington, Jack Mitchell, Vic. Pontin, John Peacock, Alan Swinburne. Middle row: Joe Freak, N. Westgarth, E. Atkinson, J. Mackeson, Bob Howe, Johny Barrow, R. Lee, N. Dodds, Davie Davis, Leslie Angus, Tom Brewis. Front row: Jack Collins, ? Richards, ? Green, ? Smith.

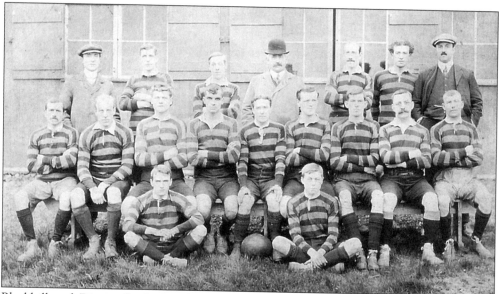

Blackhill and District Rugby Football Club, 1909-10. Back row: A.N. Burkett (secretary), W. Walton, J.W. Ridley, Dr Bratton (president), C.E. Ayton, E.C. Brown, P. Freeman (hon. treasurer). Middle row: T. Lumley, A.G. Kent, N. Sayers, J. Childs, Revd H.S. Jack (captain), E.H. Davies, E.R. Little, E.W. Stords, F. Waite. Front row: S. Carver (vice captain), E. Frere.

The Consett Iron Company Tug 'O' War team at the turn of the century. Back row: J. Struthers, J. Minnighan, H. Murphy, J. Dunne, W. Arthurs, R. Young, J. Daly. Third row: H. Donnelly, J. Heggerty, B. Mullen, T. Dunne, M. Donohue (president), D. Rafferty, J. Kempson, P. O'Brian, M. Donnelly (trainer). Second row. M. Scott, W. Lavery, M. Murray, B. Young (captain), M. Grimes, J. Lee, J. Loughran. Front row: B. Duffy, W. Dunne, P. Young.

Ready! Steady! Go! Natty Draffan (left) was well known as a foot runner during the 1920s. Here he is squaring up for a practice session.

The Annual Ladies Tennis Tournament in Consett Park in August 1941. The shortage of contesting young men for the tournament was as a result of them being away fighting for their country. This did not deter these young ladies from carrying on their tradition. Included are: Cissie Milligan, Helen (Ella) and Norah Murphy, A. Whitfield and the three McGuckin sisters.

Ten local lads thought to be taken during the 1940s or early '50s, show willing in their gardening class in school.

St Patrick's Boys' Club boxing team, 1944-45. Included are: John Donnelly, John and Gerry Burns, Gerry Armstrong, Father Ryan, Gerry Pinkney, Joe Divers, John 'Dollar' Martin, Tommy Crozier, Corrigan and Milligan.

A likely looking group of judo men. Mr Tom Howarth is the instructor.

Members of the Rose and Crown ladies darts team during the 1970s. Left to right: Mesdames Joan Robinson, Belle Emerson, Emily Bell (back), Elizabeth Carr (front), Hannah Carr and Joyce Heslop.

The darts team and trophy won by the Rose and Crown team. Among the winners were: Bernard Watson, J. McNally, R. Wilson, T. Walton, W. Tate, A. Kendall, J. Watson, A. Rushgrove, E. Bell and M. Rushgrove.

A Braes 'O' Derwent Hunt Meet at Shotley Bridge during the 1950s.

Junior Operatives at 'The Danby Fry-up' near Whitby. Young aspiring steel workers were given a six week course at Consett Technical College before embarking on this character building course. Included are: J. Dobson, J. Haley, G. Ward, P. Kelly, A. Moon, S. Gibson, P. O'Donnel, G. Glasgow, K. Britton, G. McGuire, J. Wigham, F. Scott and A. Pilchard.

A tense moment during a 'jumbles' competition. They are disputing who has got the shot as, apparently, it is a 'toucher' for both teams.

The winners of the competitions run by the Consett Park Bowling Club for 1961. They are: S. Kasher, W. Burleigh, L. Inglis, R. Smith, W. Gibson, J. Walton and J. Burns.

The weekly 'Palais De Dance' was once all the vogue during the 1930s, '40s and early '50s. From Castle's Ballroom at Catchgate to the Co-operative Dance Hall in Newmarket Street, Consett, people flocked for their entertainment. Here we have, Bob Eccles (tenor sax), Ken Maddison (clarinet) and Ken Gray entertaining the floor during the 1950s.

Consett's newly formed pipe band on parade in 1959. This was one of their first public outings, allowing members of the public to enjoy the skirl of the pipes to the marching of men.

Hughie Malone and his father Joe rose to the occasion at this St Patrick's church concert at the old Civic Hall in Middle Street in March 1956. The hall has had various names in the past, including the Palais and Daly's Music Hall.

Globe Theatre, Consett.

Resident Manager - - Mr. Lloyd Clarance.

Open all the year round.

COMEDY !
DRAMA !
REVUE !
PANTOMIME !

6-50   ‹ TWICE NIGHTLY ›   **8-50**

MOTOR BUSSES start and stop immediately opposite the Theatre to and from Stanley, Annfield Plain, Chester-le-St. Dipton, Flint Hill, Medomsley, Westwood, Castleside, Knitsley, Blackhill, Shotley-Bridge, and all intermediate stages.

— Seats may be booked by Telephone ; No. 95 Consett. —

Prices of admission including tax,

Dress Circle 1/6.   Circle 1/2.
Stalls 1/-.   Pit Stalls 8d.   Pit 5d.

The Freemasons' Arms, as many will know, was previously known as the Globe Theatre. Their simple advertisement tells it all!

Medomsley Edge Jazz Band, *c.* 1928. Community and social spirit of the developing off-shoot of the more ancient village of Medomsley is shown in the cross section of age groups here.

Eight
Celebrations

Almost every street in every town in the country had its own celebratory decorations for the Coronation of King George VI in 1937. The now demolished Dobson Street in Blackhill had its fair share of the celebrations at the time.

Wood Street in Shotley Bridge was the setting for this street party in 1935 and the occasion was the Jubilee of King George V and Queen Mary. The celebrations were such that the usual bunting was supplemented with the 'designer' bunting being hung from clothes lines from bedroom windows.

Another victory celebration took place when Martin Kearney, seen here cutting the cake, had good reason to smile as he had been a prisoner of war. The ladies in the photo who lived in Eltringham Street, Blackhill are: Mrs Gibson, Mrs Hilda Mellon, Mrs Hobson, Betty Wilson, Mrs Dewhurst, Mrs Norah Fisher, Jessie Douglas, Mrs Rose McNally and Mrs Wilson.

Blackhill 'Tin Mill' School, around 1935, when residents of nearby Hawthorn and Railway Terrace had this photograph taken in the school grounds. Among those recognised are: Mrs Newton, Mrs Brannigan, Jack and Lizzie Philips, Bob Ramsey, Mrs Allison, Mrs Hodgson, Arthur Whitfield, Mr and Mrs Moss, and Mrs Smith, to name but a few.

Crookhall Foundry celebrating V.E. Day. A sharp eye is needed to discover the only man on the photograph, Mr Harry Emmerson.

Everyone helped out at this open air party at Derwent Cottages. It was May 1945 and Victory in Europe Day and after six long years of war and hardship, at last it was all over. Although there were many shortages in food, and fancy good suppliers were in short supply, everyone helped out.

A fancy dress competition thought to be in
1937. Shotley Spa was the venue for this great
day out. Among the contestants were Mrs
Olive Clark and Rita Oxley.

Gladys Maddison was a well-known figure in
the Consett area. Gladys, whose married name
was Ford, was born in 1915 and died in 1984.
Being a talented and accomplished dancer, she
was both gold and silver medallist in the
National Dancing Teachers' Association.
Gladys was to become a dance teacher in
Blackhill for many years.

8th June, 1946

TO-DAY, AS WE CELEBRATE VICTORY, I send this personal message to you and all other boys and girls at school. For you have shared in the hardships and dangers of a total war and you have shared no less in the triumph of the Allied Nations.

I know you will always feel proud to belong to a country which was capable of such supreme effort; proud, too, of parents and elder brothers and sisters who by their courage, endurance and enterprise brought victory. May these qualities be yours as you grow up and join in the common effort to establish among the nations of the world unity and peace.

George R.I.

A celebration for a great victory, and the end to the conflict of the Second World War. Every child of school age received this message from His Majesty King George VI to mark the event.

Highgate show in Bridgehill was a lively affair during the 1950s. Above: The spectators include: Benny Wilson, William Toole and Billy Lux. The three 'Likely Lads' exercising an air of light-hearted authority on the occasion were Tommy Toole, Mark Bradley and Tommy Kelly. Below: Bobby Eccles (top hat), with Tommy Toole and Mark Bradley show the flag.

Mr J.W. Bradley, known as 'Chor' to his many friends, took a prominent part in the entertainments side of Highgate Show at Blackhill. Chor was always ready to act the fool to give pleasure to children. His mounted policeman act in a previous show was a winner.

Residents of Golden Acre in Blackhill enjoyed themselves by celebrating the Queen Elizabeth II Jubilee in 1977.

Thought to have been taken in Ridley Street, Blackhill, among the residents pictured here are those with the surnames: Peacock, McKinnel, Mitcheson, Saxty, Sieman, Colbourne, Hawkins, Eddy and Siesan.

Thought to be shortly before the Second World War, this celebration was in Blackhill. Included are: Hector McKinnel, Mr Mitcheson jnr, Mrs Postle, Mr Hawthorne, Joe Peacock, Mrs Nicholson, Mrs Young, Mrs Blemmins and Mrs Cockburn.

Mr and Mrs Thomas Hope looked far younger than their stated ages and it came as something of a shock to realise they were celebrating their Golden Anniversary on 19 December 1975. At that time Thomas Hope was seventy-three and his wife Frances was nearly seventy years of age. Mr Hope agreed that it was because of the good health that he and his wife had enjoyed, while Mrs Hope agreed that raising seven children had kept them busy. Thomas and Frances were married at the Lanchester Register Office during the Strike in 1925 and Tom worked for over fifty years for Consett Iron Company's coal pits. By 1975 Tom and Frances had over eighteen grandchildren and five great grandchildren.

Nine
Odds and Ends

As there were no paddling pools ready to hand on this day, two toddlers enjoy a splash and cool off in the bath after an exciting summer's day in 1958.

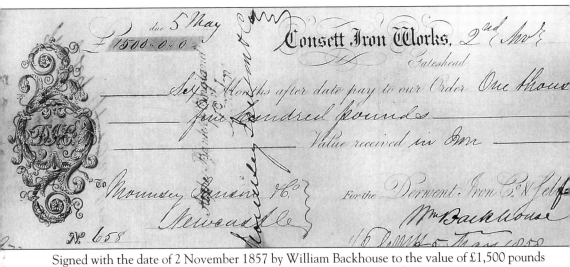

Signed with the date of 2 November 1857 by William Backhouse to the value of £1,500 pounds for payment to the Derwent Iron Company on the 5 May 1858. This was quite a vast sum in those days.

BALANCE SHEET
OF THE
CONSETT IRON COMPANY, LIMITED.

Dr.   MADE UP TO JUNE 30TH, 1885.   **Cr.**

CAPITAL AND LIABILITIES.		£	s.	d.	PROPERTY AND ASSETS.		£	s.
SHARE CAPITAL.					Property Purchase Account			
73,600 Shares— £7 10s. per Share paid	...	552,000	0	0	as per Balance Sheet made			
Creditors on Loans secured by Bond	...	200,049	14	0	up to June 30th, 1884		615,396	0
Creditors on Trade Account	...	63,162	19	8	ADDITIONS DURING YEAR			
Consett Spanish Ore Company, Limited	...	2,114	3	9	ENDED JUNE 30TH, 1885:—			
Reserve for Bad and Doubtful Debts	...	10,000	0	0	Steel Works... ... ... £25,934 19 8			
Reserve for Colliery Shorts		10,000	0	0	Purchase of Delves Farm			
					Buildings and Lands .. 4,777 0 0			
UNDIVIDED PROFIT :—							30,692	19
Returned to Shareholders,							646,089	0
March 31st, 1882, in reduc-								
tion of Paid-up Capital ... £8,355 0 0					REDUCTIONS DURING YEAR			
Balance 11,600 3 1					ENDED JUNE 30TH, 1885:—			
Amount as per last year's Report ...	...	19,955	3	1	Royalty on Coal and Clay			
		857,282	0	6	wrought out of the Com-			
Profit for year ended June					pany's Freeholds £497 0 7			
30th, 1885... ... ... £60,122 10 8					Land sold at Consett and			
Less Interim Dividend of					Blackhill 408 8 6			
5s per Share, paid Febru-								
ary 16th, 1885 ... ... 18,400 0 0								

A typical balance sheet of the Consett Iron Company, 1880.

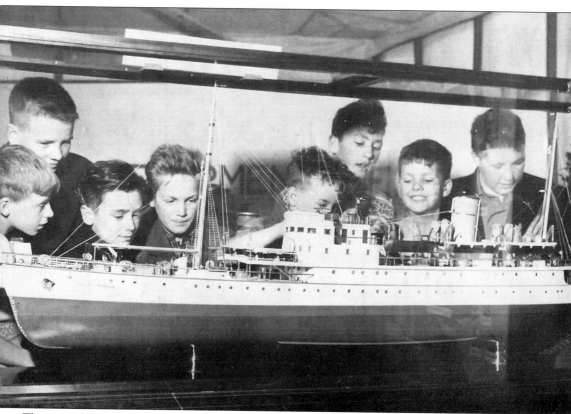

The great ships which sail the oceans are built with steel plates which at one time were made and rolled at Consett, and this fact attracted these boys to a model displayed in the company marquee at the Consett Show in 1959. At the time it was kindly loaned by Swan Hunter and Wigham Richardson of Wallsend on Tyne. It is understood to be presently a part of the collection of the Newcastle Discovery Museum, Blandford Street, Newcastle.

It was the custom at one time to place matches on the bars of inns for the use of the customers. Sometimes they were in a holder (as on the right) but to deter the greedy ones they could be inserted in the device on the left and only one could be obtained at a time - through the medium of the sharp beak of the 'bird'. Surely an odd bird, if ever there was one!

Latest findings on the working population

Irrespective of the findings of the market research experts, the following seem to be stark facts facing you and me :

Population of the United Kingdom	50,000,000
People of 65 years and older	13,000,000
Balance left to do the work	37,000,000
People of 18 years and younger	17,000,000
Balance left to do the work	20,000,000
People working for the Government	10,000,000
Balance left to do the work	10,000,000
People in the Armed Services	2,500,000
Balance left to do the work	7,500,000
People in State and Council Offices	7,300,000
Balance left to do the work	200,000
People in hospitals, lunatic asylums, pools and racing	126,000
Balance left to do the work	74,000
Spivs and others who won't work	62,000
Balance left to do the work	12,000
Persons in jail	11,998
Balance left to do the work	2

Two ! You and me—and you had better pull your ruddy socks up for I'm getting tired and fed-up of running this country alone.

                                                      (*signed*) J. F. ALLEN

The following is published without comment and in the exact form in which it was discovered. No responsibility is accepted for the accuracy of the figures quoted!

Another unusual photograph, these two rabbits adopted 'Vic' the dog after losing their mother. He proved to be a very good 'mother' except that he could not feed them. The owner took on this task by feeding the lucky orphans with bread soaked in milk or 'boily', after which they would snuggle up to Vic and go to sleep!

A new home at last for the Consett Fountain, lost from the town for many years after its removal, firstly, from Front Street, and then from Aynsley Terrace. In later years it was found in a local council depot and taken to Beamish Museum where it was restored to some of its former glory. An official unveiling ceremony was performed in 1997.

Members and guests of the Derwentdale Local History Society enjoy themselves on a visit to the Leeds Armouries in 1996.

Acknowledgements

While every effort has been made to contact and acknowledge due to copyright within this book, the Derwentdale Local History Society would like to thank those copyright holders of photographs contained within the publication where this has not been possible. Acknowledgement is offered by (alphabet):

Mr & Mrs Eric Bell, Mr Mark Bradley, Mr Tom Brewis, Mrs Susan Breen, Mr & Mrs Roy Collins, Mr & Mrs Gordon Curtis, Messrs Colin & Norman Davidson, Mr & Mrs Tommy Donnelly, Mr John Dickenson, Mr John Dobson, Mr Ollie Eastham, Mr Bob Eccles, 'Mal' Edwards, Mr R. English, Mr John Greener, Dr & Mrs J. Hamilton, Mr Ray Hardy, Mrs Muriel Howe, Mrs Howe (Corbridge), Mr & Mrs Colin Hume, Mr John Hope, Jefferson Air Photography, Mr & Mrs Bill Johnson, Mr John Lee, Mr Brian Little, Mr & Mrs Hugh Malone, Mrs R. McNally, Mr Tony McCrory, Mrs Alison McKay, Mr Dennis McKenna, Miss Ella Murphy, Mr Brian Murphy, Mrs Wendy Oughton, Mrs Mary Parker, Mr Jim Rutherford, Miss V. Smith, Mrs Patricia Tunnicliffe, Mr & Mrs Arthur Walch, Mr Eric Walls and Mr 'Tess' Wilson.

The Derwentdale Local History Society would care to thank the British Steels General Division Plc for their kind support and attention and that particularly of the teachers and staff of St Mary's Primary R.C. School, Blackhill and the staff and everyone at Remanoid Ltd. Our Society would further care to thank those members of the general public who have kindly offered help and advice on much of the subject matter within this publication without which some detail would have been sadly lost to future generations.